Dear Parent:
Your child's love of reading starts here!

Every child learns to read in a different way and at his or her own speed. Some go back and forth between reading levels and read favorite books again and again. Others read through each level in order. You can help your young reader improve and become more confident by encouraging his or her own interests and abilities. From books your child reads with you to the first books he or she reads alone, there are I Can Read Books for every stage of reading:

SHARED READING
Basic language, word repetition, and whimsical illustrations, ideal for sharing with your emergent reader

BEGINNING READING
Short sentences, familiar words, and simple concepts for children eager to read on their own

READING WITH HELP
Engaging stories, longer sentences, and language play for developing readers

READING ALONE
Complex plots, challenging vocabulary, and high-interest topics for the independent reader

ADVANCED READING
Short paragraphs, chapters, and exciting themes for the perfect bridge to chapter books

I Can Read Books have introduced children to the joy of reading since 1957. Featuring award-winning authors and illustrators and a fabulous cast of beloved characters, I Can Read Books set the standard for beginning readers.

A lifetime of discovery begins with the magical words **"I Can Read!"**

Visit www.icanread.com for information
on enriching your child's reading experience.

Library of Congress catalog card number: 2011938180
ISBN 978-0-06-208609-9 (trade bdg.)—ISBN 978-0-06-208608-2 (pbk.)

12 13 14 15 16   SCP   10 9 8 7 6 5 4 3 2 1   ❖   First Edition

I Can Read!

BEGINNING
1
READING

Dixie
and the
School Trip

story by Grace Gilman

pictures by Sarah McConnell

HARPER

An Imprint of HarperCollinsPublishers

"Guess what, Dixie?"

said Emma one morning.

"I'm going to see dinosaurs today!"

Dixie was surprised.

She let out a yelp.

How could Emma see dinosaurs?

Dinosaurs lived long ago.

"Don't worry." Emma laughed.

"They aren't real.

I am going to the dinosaur museum

with my school!"

"There's the bus," said Emma.

She hurried out the door.

Dixie yipped. She yapped.

Going to the museum

sounded like fun.

Dixie wanted to go, too.

Emma waved good-bye to her mom.

She did not see Dixie

jump into the bus!

Emma sat down.

Dixie sat with her.

"Dixie!" cried Emma.

Dixie licked Emma's face.

"Oh well," said Emma.

"I guess you're coming with us!"

At the museum, a woman met the class
by a big dinosaur model.
"This is Ms. Digg,"
said Emma's teacher.
"She is a dinosaur expert."

Emma was amazed.

"Look, Dixie," she said.

"A real dinosaur expert!"

"I hunt for clues to learn about how
dinosaurs lived," said Ms. Digg.
"I've searched for dinosaur bones
all over the world!"

"Did you hear that, Dixie?"
said Emma.

"One day, I'm going to search
for dinosaur bones, too."

Dixie yipped.

She yapped.

She had an idea!

When no one was looking,

Dixie took a bone.

She hid it under a bench.

Now Emma could search

for dinosaur bones, too!

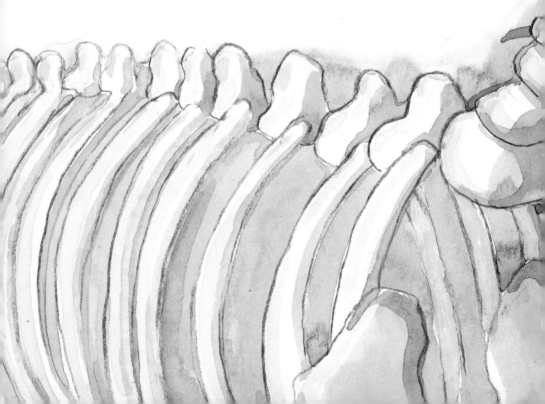

Dixie sneaked back to Emma.

She was listening to Ms. Digg.

"Did you know that some dinosaurs

never ate meat?" said Ms. Digg.

"Wow," said Emma.
She was so busy listening
she did not see Dixie
hide another bone!

Ms. Digg took the class to a room
with lots of dinosaur models.
"Dinosaurs didn't just
walk on land," she said.
"Some could fly and swim!"

Dixie stole another bone.

She put this one in

a dinosaur's mouth!

21

"Experts keep journals about their discoveries," said Ms. Digg. "Now it's your turn to write about what you learned today."

Emma drew a flying dinosaur.

"Now I want to draw a bone," she said.

Dixie was so happy.

She had brought one with her!

"Dixie!" cried Emma.

"Where did this come from?

We have to put it back."

Emma and Dixie left the room
where the others were working.
They turned left.
They turned right.
"Where does this bone belong?"
said Emma.

Dixie yipped softly.

She did not want Emma to be upset.

Then Dixie had an idea.

She pawed at Emma's journal.

"Hey," said Emma.

"There are clues in here
about where we've been.

It's almost like a map!"

Emma and Dixie went to the room

with the dinosaur statues.

There, she found another bone Dixie hid.

She found another bone

in the room with all the plant eaters.

She found another bone

in a dinosaur's mouth.

Emma gave all the bones to Ms. Digg.

"I'm sorry," she said.

"Dixie didn't mean to steal these."

Ms. Digg was nice about it.

"Stealing bones is bad,"

she told Dixie.

"But you two can be proud!"

"Why?" said Emma.

"You used good clues to search
for bones all over," said Ms. Digg.
"I'd say you and Dixie have become
real dinosaur experts!"